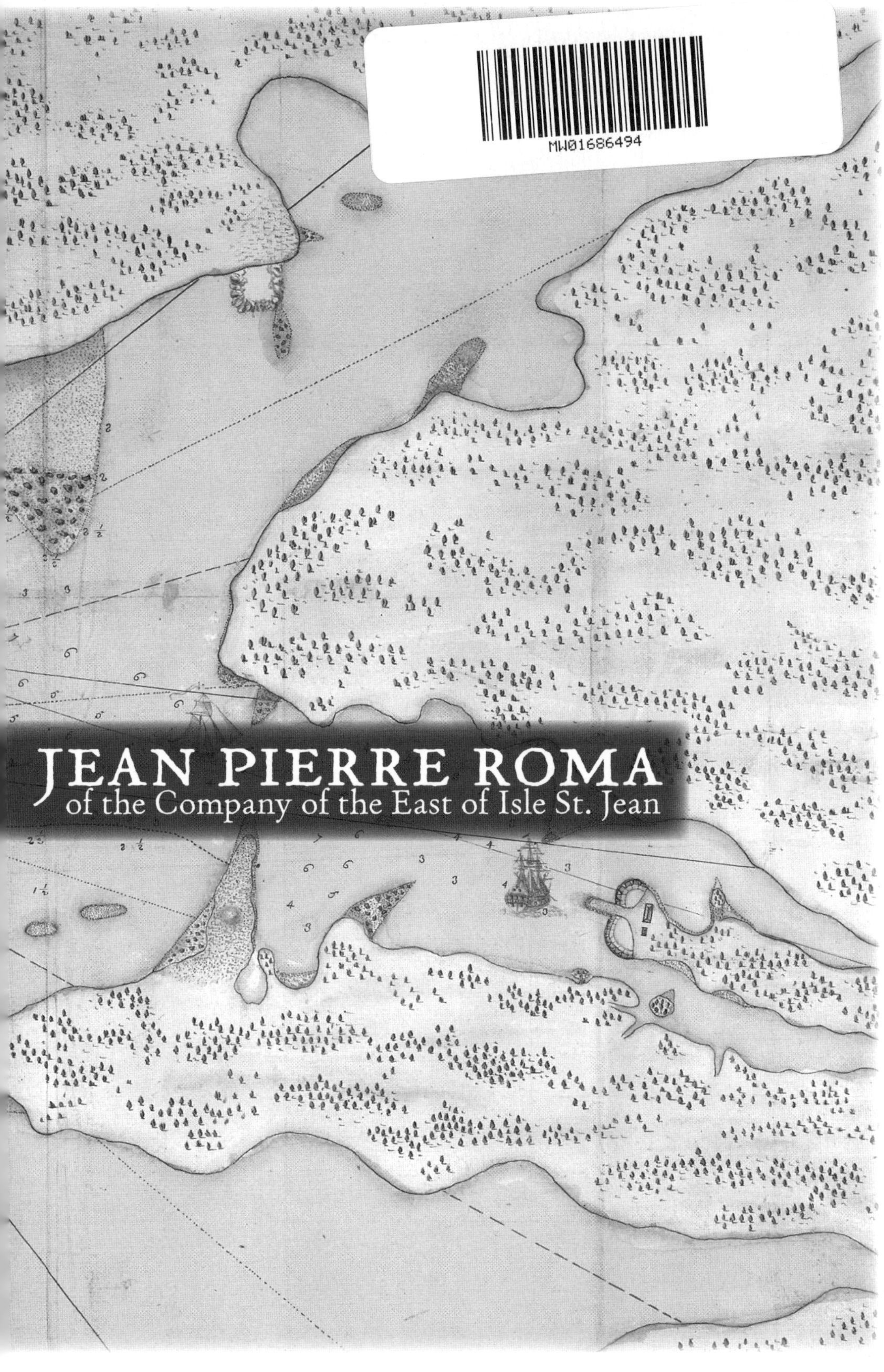

JEAN PIERRE ROMA
of the Company of the East of Isle St. Jean

Jean Pierre Roma

of the Company of the East of Isle St. Jean

Jill MacLean

Acorn Press / Three Rivers Roma Inc.
2005

Jean Pierre Roma of the Company of the East of Isle St. Jean
Text © 2005 by Jill MacLean
ISBN 1-894838-15-7

Jean Pierre Roma of the Company of the East of Isle St. Jean was originally published in 1977 by the Prince Edward Island Heritage Foundation, as part of the Cornelius Howatt Commemorative Series (No. 4).

Design: Matthew MacKay
Printing: Hignell Book Printing

The Acorn Press gratefully acknowledges the support of the Prince Edward Island Council of the Arts. Three Rivers Roma Inc. gratefully acknowledges the support of the Prince Edward Island Department of Community and Cultural Affairs' Cultural Development Program.

Library and Archives Canada Cataloguing in Publication

MacLean, Jill
Jean Pierre Roma of the Company of the East of Isle St. Jean / by Jill MacLean.

Includes bibliographical references.
ISBN 1-894838-15-7
1. Roma, Jean Pierre. 2. Compagnie de l'Est de l'Île Saint-Jean. 3. Prince Edward Island—History—To 1873. 4. Prince Edward Island—Emigration and immigration—History—18th century. 5. France—Emigration and immigration—History—18th century. 6. Prince Edward Island—Biography. I. Title.

FC306.R64M32 2005 971.7'01 C2005-902383-X

ACORN PRESS

PO Box 22024
Charlottetown, Prince Edward Island
Canada C1A 9J2
www.acornpresscanada.com

Three Rivers Roma Inc.
P.O. Box 758
Montague, Prince Edward Island
Canada C0A 1R0
www.romapei.com

I am deeply indebted to Mr Frank Korvemaker, whose encouragement and enthusiasm fostered my interest in Jean Pierre Roma. In addition, I am very grateful for the help I have received from historians on staff at the Fortress of Louisbourg National Historic Park.

—*Jill MacLean*

NATIONAL MONUMENT COMMEMORATING JEAN PIERRE ROMA,
ERECTED IN 1936

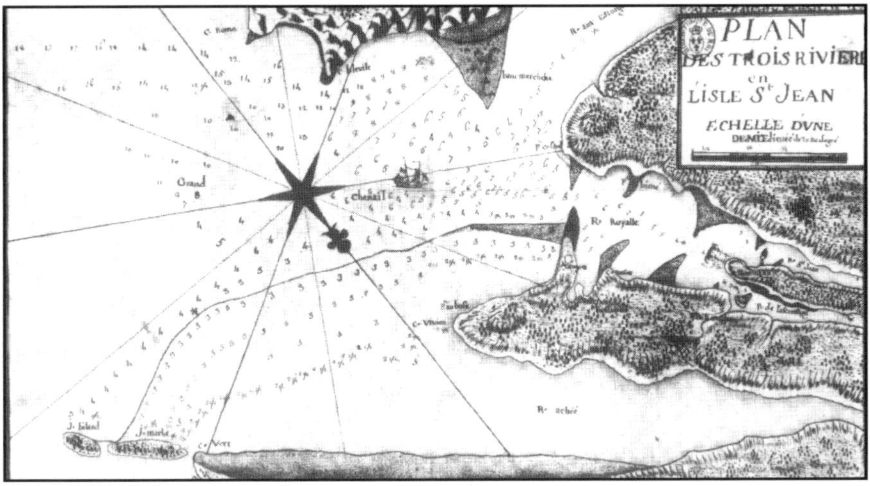

Contents

Foreword

We thank the author, Jill MacLean, and original publisher, the Prince Edward Island Heritage Foundation, for their generosity in granting us full rights to publish again this important history of Jean Pierre Roma. When they produced this monograph in 1977 as Number 4 of the Cornelius Howatt Commemorative Series, they could not have foreseen today's developments at the site that Roma called Trois Rivières.

It is with enthusiasm that now in 2005 we produce this new edition to honour Jean Pierre Roma and to encourage visitors to the trails, buildings, and activities on the historic point of land between Prince Edward Island's Montague and Brudenell Rivers, now called Roma at Three Rivers.

Three Rivers Roma Inc.
www.romapei.com

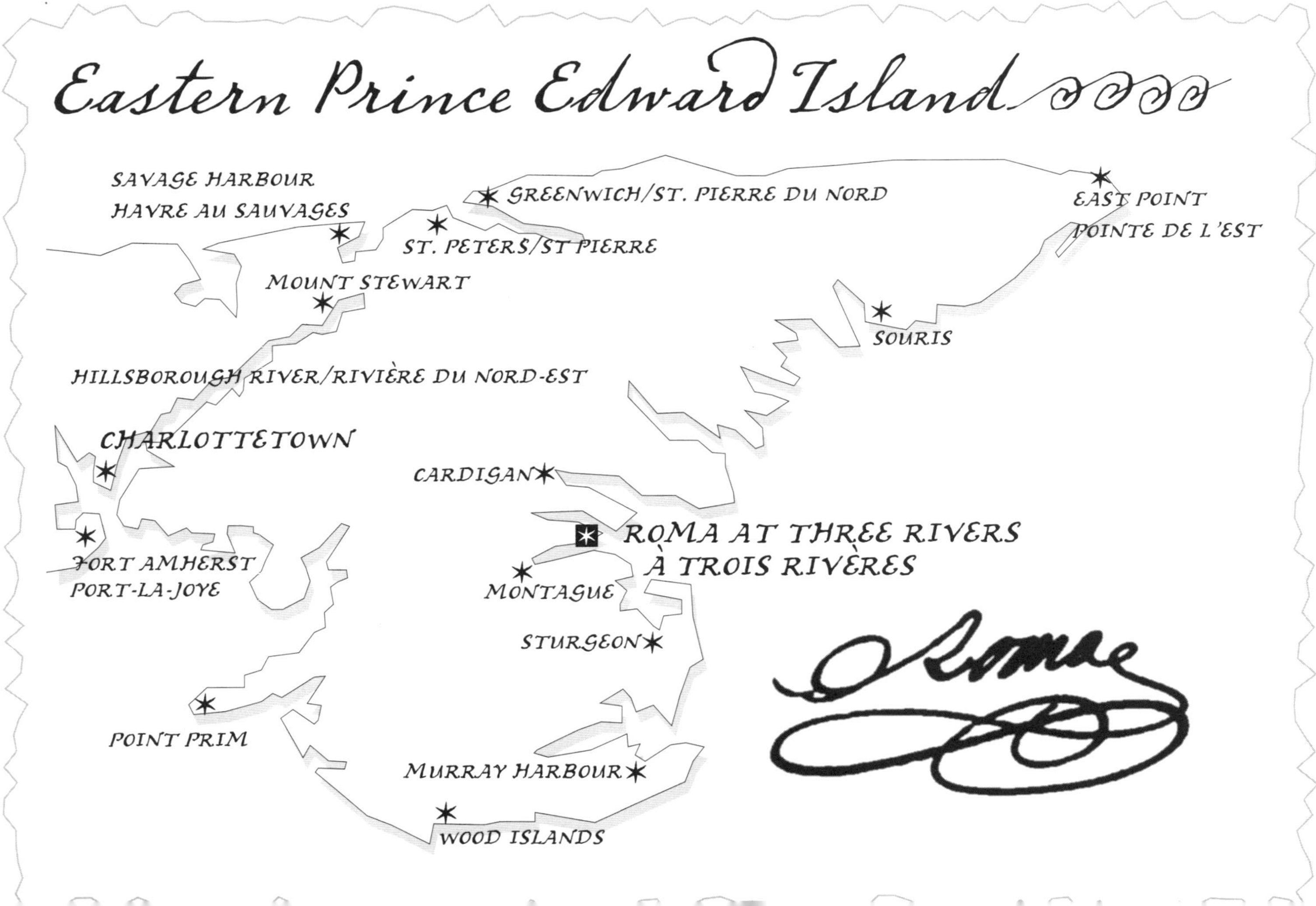
Eastern Prince Edward Island
SAVAGE HARBOUR
HAVRE AU SAUVAGES
GREENWICH/ST. PIERRE DU NORD
ST. PETERS/ST PIERRE
EAST POINT
POINTE DE L'EST
MOUNT STEWART
SOURIS
HILLSBOROUGH RIVER/RIVIÈRE DU NORD-EST
CHARLOTTETOWN
CARDIGAN
ROMA AT THREE RIVERS
À TROIS RIVÈRES
FORT AMHERST
PORT-LA-JOYE
MONTAGUE
STURGEON
POINT PRIM
MURRAY HARBOUR
WOOD ISLANDS

Glossary of Place Names

Isle St. Jean	St. John's Island, renamed Prince Edward Island
Isle Royal	Cape Breton Island
Trois Rivières	Three Rivers, now Brudenell Point
Port la Joye	The French capital of Isle St. Jean, near Fort Amherst
St. Pierre	St. Peter's, Prince Edward Island
Rivière du Nord-Est	North East River, now the Hillsborough River
Havre aux Sauvages	Savage Harbour
Pointe de l'Est	East Point
Rivière des Esturgeons	Sturgeon River
Port Dauphin	St. Ann's, Cape Breton
Martinique, Guadeloupe, and St. Domingue (Haiti)	French islands in the West Indies

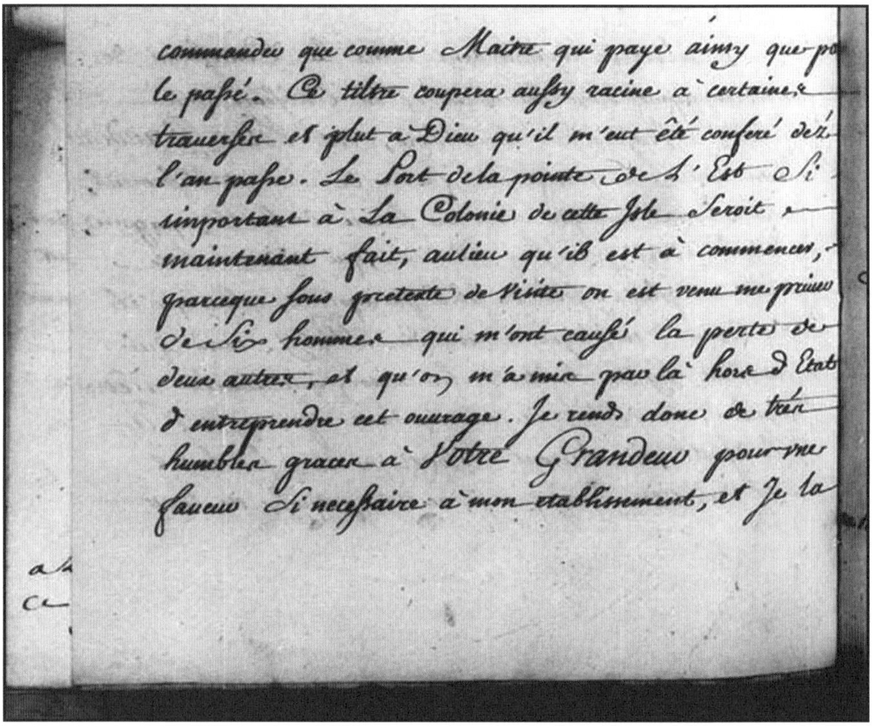

commander que comme Maitre qui paye ainsy que p
le passé. Ce titre coupera aussy racine à certaines
traverses et plut a Dieu qu'il m'eut été conferé dès
l'an passé. Le Port dela pointe de l'Est si
important à La Colonie de cette Isle seroit
maintenant fait, aulieu qu'il est à commencer,
parceque sous pretexte de Visite on est venu me priver
de six hommes qui m'ont causé la perte de
deux autres, et qu'on m'a mis par là hors d'Etat
d'entreprendre cet ouvrage. Je rends donc de très
humbles graces à Votre Grandeur pour une
faveur si necessaire à mon etablissement, et je la

ROMA'S HANDWRITING FROM A LETTER, 1733

Introduction

Jean Pierre Roma has been dead for more than two centuries. He was never famous. His endeavours came to nothing, and the ashes of his settlement are buried under the red soil of Prince Edward Island. Yet he cannot be dismissed as a failure.

He was a complex man, opinionated, energetic, and strong-willed, meticulously honest and woefully tactless. Trained in trade and commerce, he worshipped order and logic. Always restless, he was driven by the plans and projects that whirled in his brain, for he was a man of vision, a man who dreamed dreams. During the 1730s, at Trois Rivières, these dreams took on concrete form: painstakingly hewn from the wilderness, solidly constructed in wood and stone, his little kingdom grew. He would found a utopia for colonist and merchant, to the glory of His Majesty Louis XV of France — and to the glory of Monsieur Roma himself.

Roma wanted his establishment to be the lynchpin of a busy and profitable commerce. In exchange for lumber from the forests of Isle St. Jean and fish from the northern coastal waters would come West Indian sugar, molasses, and coffee, which in turn could be traded for biscuits and flour in Quebec. When Trois Rivières became self-supporting, any excess produce raised by Roma's settlers could be sold to the ever-hungry garrison at Louisbourg. By shipping cargoes of fish, dried and salted, to France, he would obtain the manufactured goods the colonies could not provide.[1]

On paper this was an excellent scheme, but it was dogged by ill-fortune from the start, despite Roma's fierce determination to succeed.

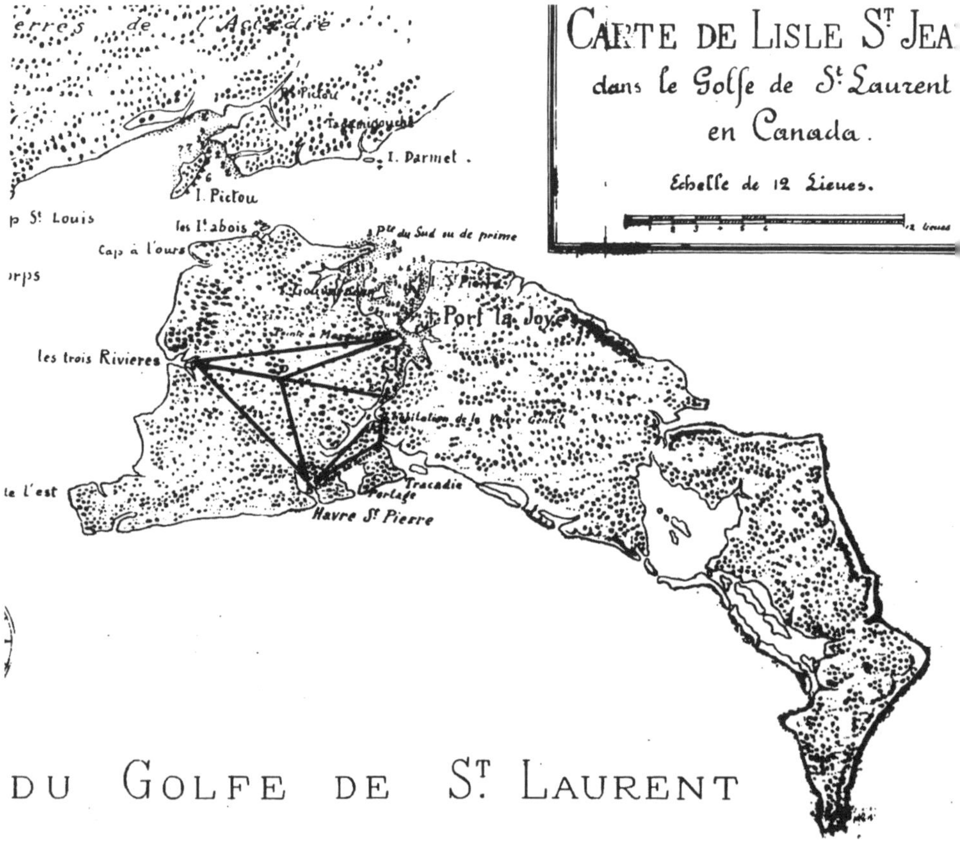

AN EARLY MAP OF PRINCE EDWARD ISLAND.
NOTE: FRENCH MAPS OF THAT TIME SHOW NORTH
AT THE BOTTOM OF THE PAGE.
THE STRAIGHT LINES SHOW THE ROADS BUILT BY ROMA.

The Founding of a Company (1731–1732)

When was Roma born? Where did he spend his childhood? How did he develop an interest in New France? Unfortunately, information about his early life is tantalizingly scanty, and many questions must remain unanswered. According to the censuses recorded in Isle St. Jean in 1734 and 1735, Roma was born in Bordeaux, probably before the turn of the century. In 1731 he was described as a merchant of Paris. And, in 1741, writing to the Minister of the Marine in France, Roma himself provided a recapitulation of his youthful career, a career that even then did not run smoothly. He recalled

> ... that the arrangements of M. Desmarets ruined my fortune in 1715; that when the Duc d'Orléans returned the concession on the southern coast of St. Domingue to the King's domain, he cut short my activities there which would have restored my fortune; that M. de Cambis, His Majesty's ambassador to the court of Turin, was unwilling for me to accept a considerable and very honourable position in the service of the King of Sardinia in 1726....[2]

These setbacks, however, did not deter Roma from seeking new adventures, or from endeavouring to make his mark in the busy world of commerce. In 1731 he took the first step towards Trois Rivières when he journeyed from Paris to Fontainebleau. This elegant palace provided a setting as different from the wilderness of Isle St. Jean as could be imagined, for through its vast halls and immaculate gardens strutted the powdered and perfumed members of a sycophantic and doomed nobility. Under the auspices of Louis X, and Maurepas, his Minister of the Marine (responsible for colonial affairs), four men gathered there in July 1731. They were Claude Cottard from Rouen, Joseph du Bocage from LeHavre, Joseph Narcis and Jean Pierre Roma from Paris, and on July 17 they signed the letter of concession that was to alter Roma's future so radically.

The tenuous link between Fontainebleau and a tiny island far across the windswept Atlantic was forged by European wars and rivalries. In 1713 the War of the Spanish Succession had ended with the Treaty of Utrecht, whereby England was awarded sovereignty over peninsular Acadia, Newfoundland, and the Hudson's Bay territory, leaving to France only Isle St. Jean and Isle Royale in the Gulf of St. Lawrence

A FRENCH SCHOONER, OR "GOELETTE"

(as well as Quebec, Louisiana, and the French West Indies). By 1720, construction had begun on the mighty fortress of Louisbourg. Beyond its rocky shores a wary eye could be trained upon the English; to its wharves and warehouses came merchant vessels from Quebec, France, New England, and the Indies; and from its fish-flakes wafted the reek of drying cod. Built on a bog at enormous expense, it was believed unconquerable by Parisians and New Englanders alike — a myth shattered twice in its brief history.

The Acadians' rich lands in the Minas Basin were now under British domination, however ineffective this domination was in actuality. At first the French government tried to persuade the Acadians to move to Isle Royale. When this manoeuvre failed, attention was directed to Isle St. Jean as an alternate site. In 1719 Port la Joye was founded by the Comte de St. Pierre's company, which was declared bankrupt five years later, leaving the island deserted again except for a few fishermen and a handful of tenacious Acadian farmers. To attract further Acadian migration and to prevent the English from stealing the island from under their noses, the Louisbourg officials sent a garrison of twenty-five men and an ensign under de Pensens to Port la Joye in 1726. In 1730 the Comte de St. Pierre's grant was revoked, bringing the island back into the Royal domain. Rather than renting the land, the inhabitants could now own it, which to the land-hungry peasants was a far more agreeable state of affairs. By 1732, the population had increased to 347, clustered in the settlements of Port la Joye, Rivière du Nord-Est, Havre aux Sauvages, St. Pierre, Tracadie, Malpeque, and Pointe de l'Est.[3]

By no means were all the colonists self-supporting, so assistance was furnished by the Acadians on the mainland and by Louisbourg. Moreover, the garrison, inadequately fed on salt beef and inadequately housed under leaking roofs, regarded Port la Joye as the end of the world and longed for the rowdy taverns of Louisbourg. But in official circles there flourished high, if ill-founded, hopes that Isle St. Jean would become a dependable food source for Louisbourg, providing the cattle and grain that could not be raised in the marshes surrounding the fortress.

Undoubtedly the French government had this situation in mind when the Company of the East of Isle St. Jean was formed in 1731 at Fontainebleau. In the letters of concession a vast feudal estate was created at Trois Rivières on the eastern end of the island (the lands drained by the present-day Cardigan, Brudenell, and Montague Rivers). The King reserved mining and judicial rights, and claimed any oak trees suitable for shipbuilding and any territory needed for the building of forts, batteries, and parade grounds. Apart from these restrictions, the concessionaires could "rent out the said land without being required to pay any sums of money to the King or his successors." They had the right of patronage of one or more stone churches and could construct such mills as were deemed necessary, and also were permitted to build fishing scaffolds and storehouses on the northern shore of the island (outside their concession), land being granted on the basis of the number of boats maintained there.

The duties of the four merchants were outlined: to render homage (although not to pay rents) to the government in Louisbourg in whose jurisdiction they were situated; to send to Trois Rivières eighty settlers in 1732 and thirty every following year, with the necessary livestock and tools; to keep the land cleared and maintained, and to provide roads for the settlers. If the conditions were disregarded, the concession would revert to the Royal domain; otherwise it would be held by Cottard, du Bocage, Narcis, and Roma, their heirs and trustees, in perpetuity.[4]

In view of the failure of several previous grants of this type in Isle St. Jean and elsewhere, it seems a pity the French Court saw fit to establish yet another. In one fell swoop it removed ownership of some of the best lands and harbours of the island from the reach of the Acadians — and from the reach of Roma's settlers.

The new company wanted to send a handful of workmen to Trois Rivières in 1731 to make ready for Roma's arrival the following year.[5] Just a month after the signing of the letter of concession, Roma was in conflict with an admiralty official in Le Havre about the embarkation of a crew member. The quarrel was settled by the Minister of the Marine in Versailles,[6] the first of many such peace-making efforts on his part in the next few years. Roma's ship was able finally to set sail, but due to "contrary winds, and other mishaps," it had to turn back. By then the season was well-advanced, so it was not until the spring of 1732 that a little fleet departed for Louisbourg: one vessel with "wine, whiskey, and other effects" from Bordeaux, a second with the fishermen from Bayonne, and a third with *engagés* (workers signed up for a three-year term) from Granville and Honfleur.[7] The crossing was uneventful. On Friday, June 6, Roma appeared before the Superior Council in its damp, scantily furnished chamber in the chateau at Louisbourg. (The rich red fabrics and royal portraits seen in today's reconstruction of Louisbourg had not been acquired by 1732.)[8] He had been granted power of attorney for the Company the previous November in Rouen, and thus on his behalf and that of his fellow concessionaires, he swore "in a loud voice" faith and homage to his sovereign lord the King. As was customary, his oath of allegiance was given "without sword or spurs, bareheaded, and on bended knee" (an unusual position for Roma). The Council afterwards ordered the insertion of the letters of concession in the Louisbourg registry.[9]

Roma met with some of the local merchants during the next few days, among them the wealthy Joseph Lartigue, a member of the Superior Council.[10] But the impatient Roma did not linger long at the fortress; by the middle of June, he had commenced his project at Trois Rivières.

Great Beginnings (1732–1734)

Inadvertently, Roma left a complete picture of his accomplishments during the next two years. In the autumn of 1734, oppressed by the failure of his French colleagues to support him financially, he produced a lengthy justification of his program, including a summary of his plans for Isle St. Jean and a list of the work done in the preceding twenty-six months.[11] These documents prove conclusively that Roma was no dilettante or mere figurehead, but had been involved in all aspects of the work, planning and recording every detail, overseeing and encouraging his two hundred workmen, and economizing wherever possible within the limits of his grand design.

He located his settlement on a promontory between two rivers, on one of the best harbours of the island. After lowering the steep sides of the cape, he constructed a forty-five-foot-long jetty of rocks weighing up to eight hundred pounds each, which must have been a backbreaking task with the primitive tools at his disposal. Six thousand trees were felled and sawn up for firewood, and the stumps levered from the ground. According to the account, "some of them were so heavy that ten, twelve or even fifteen men were required to move them." The cleared land was then levelled "to prevent accumulation of stagnant water" and also "to improve the appearance of the area," for Roma thought his employees would be content with lower wages if the settlement was made attractive.

In the clearing rose nine wooden buildings, constructed of upright posts caulked with moss and coated with clay. This architectural style was called *piquet*,[12] and, although unprepossessing, was sturdy and weatherproof.

The two largest buildings, each eighty feet long, were the Company House, where Roma and his family lived, and the fishermen's house. Smaller dwellings were provided for the craftsmen, the ships' officers and crews, and the Company employees. Three other structures served as a bakery, a forge, and a stable (the latter complete with dovecote, three cattle and two horses, although the horses were of little use, being "insufficiently fed"). The buildings included storerooms and workshops, and were heated by a total of thirteen fireplaces, in which logs blazed for seven months of the year.

Springs supplied the settlers with fresh water. During the two-year period, more than 1,200 barrels were consumed for drinking, launder-

REMAINS OF A BAKERY OR FORGE UNEARTHED IN 1968-70

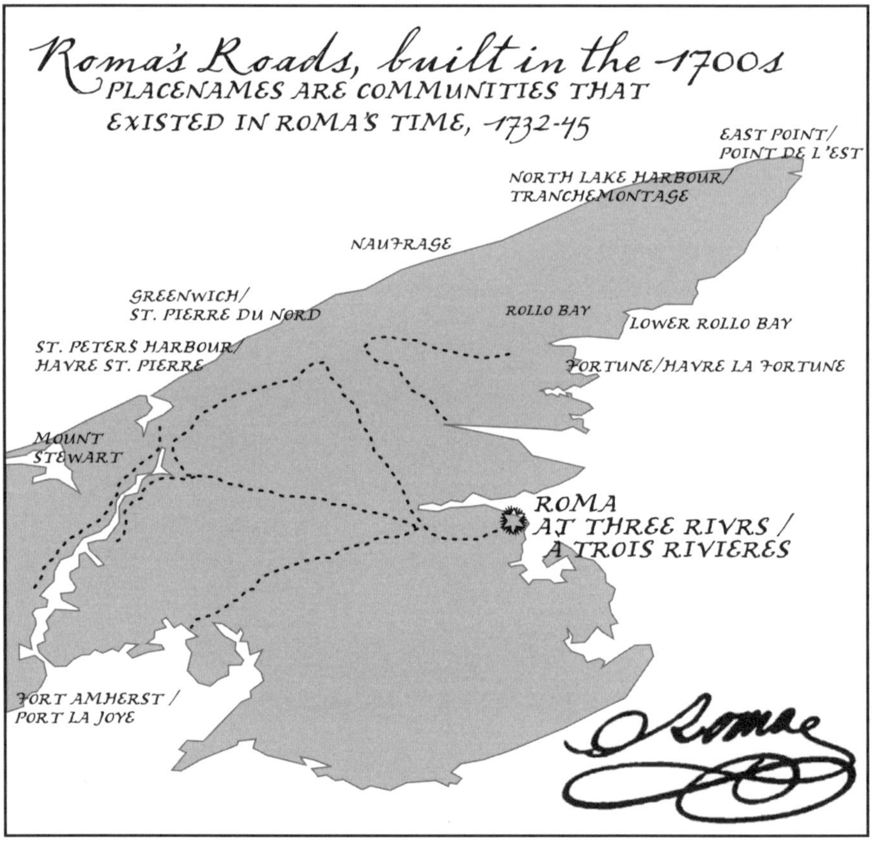

ing, beer-making, and watering the livestock. Probably very little was directed towards personal cleanliness, not a priority in the 18th century.

Cabbages and turnips grew in eight small gardens, with picket fences to prevent the pigs from rooting out the produce. Fenced also were the two half-acre fields, one sown in wheat, the other in peas. More trees were cut down along the shoreline on either side of the cape to make the coast easier to defend and, more prosaically, to destroy the bloodthirsty mosquitoes that flourished in the woods.

The extremes of temperature forced Roma to the expense of an underground storage cellar. Its excavation was undertaken in the winter, when the ground was frozen, and was "as difficult as digging into solid rock." One door opened on to a small quay on the shore, so cargoes could be loaded and unloaded directly. The second door, twenty feet from the Company house, was "under supervision at all times" — apparently not everyone was as honest as Roma.

The peace of the forest was soon shattered by Roma's road-building crews. Rough trails to the nearby rivers facilitated fishing, hunting, and hay-making. Building temporary cabins for shelter as they went, nineteen men laboured for nineteen days in the dead of winter to hack a path to St. Pierre, the fishing harbour on the north shore, thus eliminating the twenty-two-league sea journey. And, as a precaution in case of war with the English, a trail was opened between Trois Rivières and the disgruntled garrison at Port la Joye. In Roma's words, "This road is not as well worked as the other one... most of the trees lying on the ground across the road have been left where they lie, since it is easy enough to step over them."

In May 1733, the Minister formally approved Roma's concession on the harbour at St. Pierre, "in order to establish the necessary sheds and vessels for fishing."[13] It would seem that Roma had taken this permission for granted, because ten of his *chaloupes* had fished there the preceding summer and he had supplied the fifty-five fishermen with salt, bread, brandy, molasses, and wine. His carpenters erected a number of cabins and fish-drying racks, a cellar, and a building eighty-two feet by twenty-three feet, with the usual fenced garden. At St. Pierre work was completed on the seventy-ton vessel *St. Jean*, which plied between St. Pierre and Trois Rivières with cargoes of cod, 5,000 quintals in all in the twenty-six months. (A *quintal* equals 112 pounds.) This ship also made at least one voyage to Quebec. And on the harbour's sandy shores the Company schooners and fishing boats were careened, caulked, and repaired.

1700S-STYLE BUILDINGS NOW (IN 2005) OCCUPYING THE SITE OF ROMA'S SETTLEMENT AT THREE RIVERS

In addition to the tasks already described there were the day-to-day chores of cooking and baking, caring for the sick, feeding the poultry and cattle, and keeping the office records. "The Company has been served by people who have had no time to get bored," was Roma's succinct conclusion. But not everyone at Trois Rivières was as energetic and productive as the director. From all his employees (thirty-nine *engagés*, three ships' crews, twenty-four seasonal workers, twenty-three Basques, and several Norman fishermen), Roma calculated to have received the equivalent amount of work of only twenty-six men over the twenty-six-month period. Absence at sea, involvement in fishing and shipbuilding, sickness, and death could legitimately account for some of the discrepancy — desertion, feigned illness, and plain laziness the rest.

In spite of this, a monumental amount had been accomplished, for which Roma was quick to claim the credit. He explained at the end of his document how he had selected the most suitable workmen for each task, and had improved their efficiency by furnishing them with new tools. To save time and money, he had planned each operation in advance, and then supervised its implementation. Finally, he had been careful to combine work with pleasure. Singing, feasting, and dancing had given the weary settlers welcome respite from the grinding drudgery of creating a home in the wilderness, and no doubt equally welcome respite from the ubiquitous Roma, whose driving ambition and unrelenting demands for perfection must have been difficult for lesser mortals to bear.

Feuds and Finances (1732–1737)

The first twenty-six months at Trois Rivières saw the establishment of a flourishing little community, where crops were harvested, fish caught and salted, and goods traded with distant ports. These achievements, products of Roma's industry and vision, were unfortunately marred by less creditable events, products of his pride and intolerance. He was beset by problems spiritual (recalcitrant clergy) and temporal (lack of money).

To start with, he was not on speaking terms with Robert Potier Dubuisson, who, as sub-delegate of the Intendant and keeper of the King's stores on Isle St. Jean, had powers second only to those of the commandant. According to his contemporaries, Dubuisson was an honest, humane, and hard-working man,[14] yet Roma was harshly critical of him. It is hard to say to what extent Dubuisson reciprocated or deserved such animosity. Roma's high-handed attitude may well have irritated a man who had already laboured for ten years on the island and could be expected to know what he was doing. Dubuisson, for instance, probably considered he was only doing his job when he spent two months at St. Pierre in the autumn of 1732 settling disputes between Roma's employees and the local inhabitants.[15] To Roma, however, this move doubtless smacked of censure and interference.

Therefore it must be remembered that the following account is based on Roma's writings[16] —and he was far from an unprejudiced witness. He managed to bring an aura of backstairs intrigue to the feud by hinting that he had unwittingly disrupted various black-market dealings of Dubuisson's. "Besides, my enterprise had several secret enemies, to some of whom Sieur Dubuisson was strongly attached," he said. Apparently the sub-delegate tried to entice away Roma's gardener and threatened with prison one of his ship's captains. He also decided against Roma in a lawsuit concerning payment of a boat hull (for Dubuisson had the power to hear civil and criminal cases). But supposedly Roma strove to forget these "little manoeuvres" when, in December 1732, Dubuisson and his daughter Louise were forced by ice to put into Trois Rivières on their way back from Louisbourg. Roma's hospitality on this occasion was rewarded by further discord.

The Company had provided two priests to minister to its settlers. Roma suggested there was not much to choose between them, for one

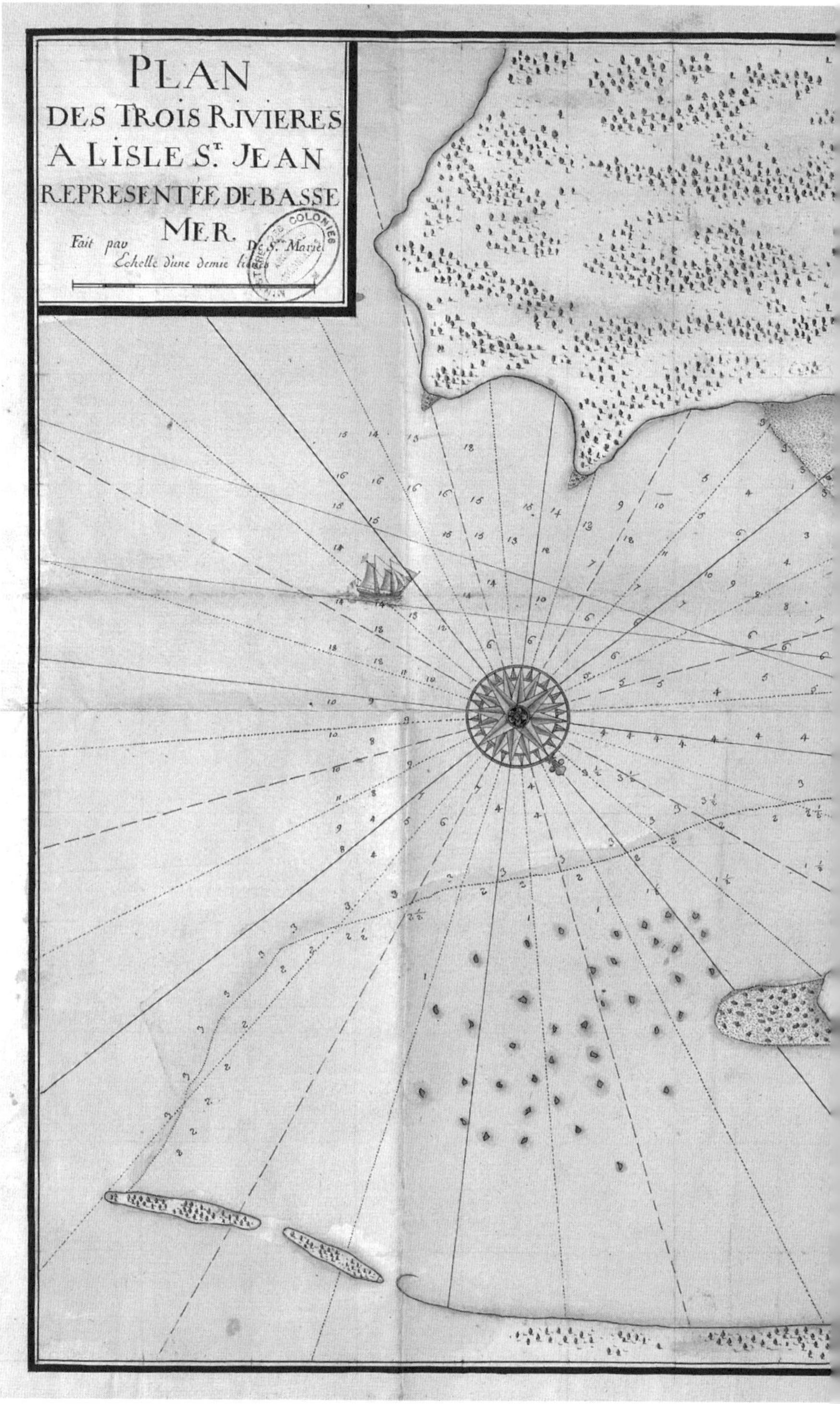

DETAIL FROM A PLAN OF TROIS RIVIÈRES, POSSIBLY BA
NORTH IS AT THE BOTTOM OF THE CHART. THE TIP OF PA
BOUGHTON ISLAND FRAM

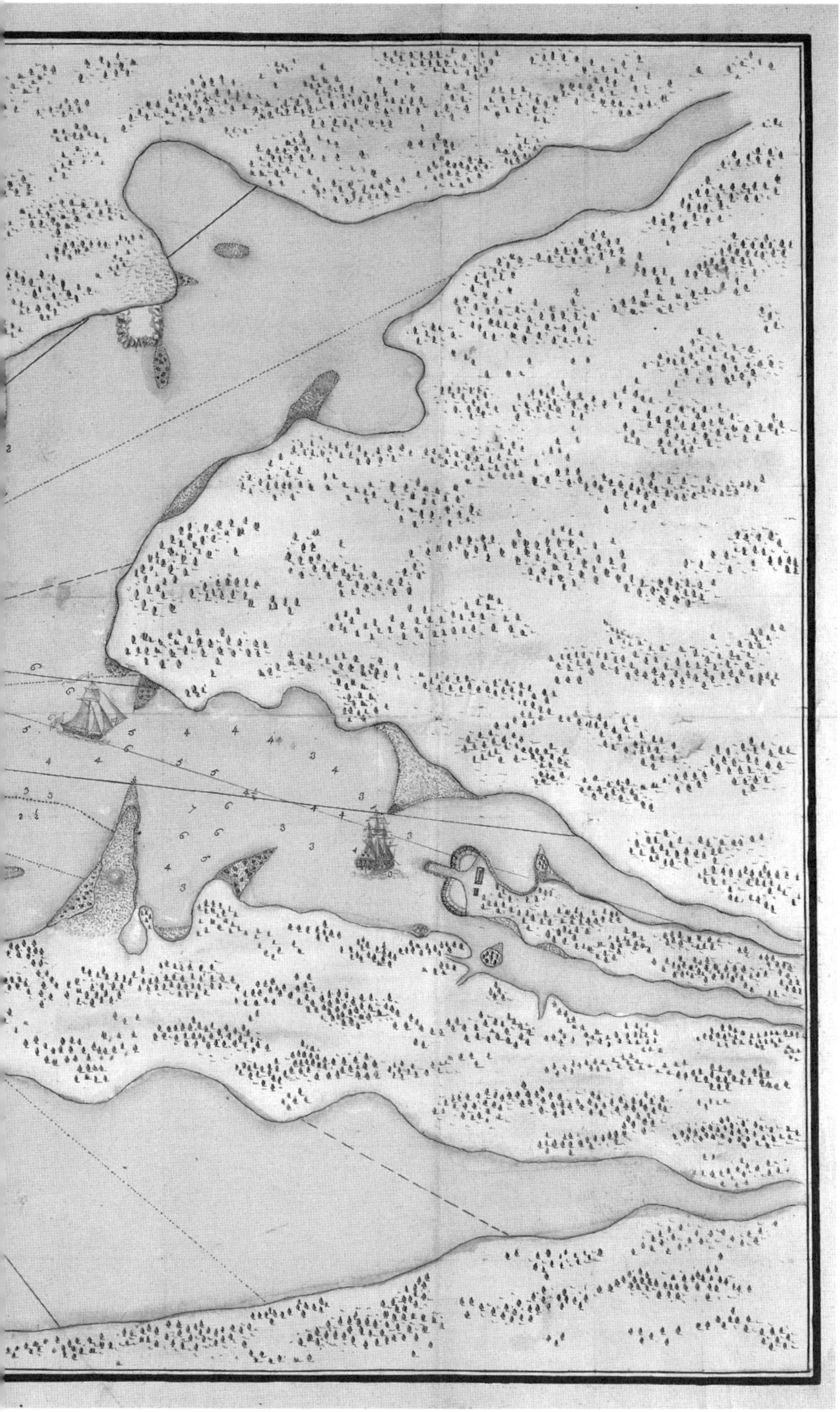

ORIGINAL BY ROMA. FOLLOWING PERIOD CONVENTION,
LAND IS LOCATED AT UPPER LEFT AND THE SOUTH EDGE OF
WER REGION OF THE MAP.

was an Irish drunkard and the other a Parisian troublemaker. The second, Abbé de Bierne by name, believed all work should cease on Sundays and feast days. To the pragmatic Roma, the urgent needs of his settlement took precedence over religious observances. During the sub-delegate's stay, de Bierne and Dubuisson took long walks upon the ice, after which the priest became so offensive in his manner that the unity of the little settlement was disrupted. Predictably this made Roma very angry.

The inevitable confrontation between priest and director occurred in April. They were two equally obdurate men, and it must have been a quarrel of resounding proportions. De Bierne claimed he was answerable to divine authority rather than to Roma's, which was too firmly grounded in things of this earth for the priest. Unable to tolerate such a flagrant flouting of his rule, Roma was ungentlemanly enough to point out all the priest's various failings, in particular accusing de Bierne of spreading dissension among the staff. Then, "furious at the conduct of a priest whose person is worthy of the utmost contempt,"[17] Roma dismissed de Bierne, not troubling to phrase the dismissal with any degree of tact.

Highly insulted by such cavalier treatment, the priest took up residence with the sub-delegate in Port la Joye, receiving sympathy and support from Dubuisson's unmarried sister, Marie Anne. Shortly afterwards the Irish chaplain joined them, discharged "for having almost killed the household while drunk." Dubuisson packed both clerics off to Louisbourg, where their cause was espoused by Zacarie Caradec, Father Superior of the Recollets, in Roma's view "a little man, vain and violent." De Bierne returned to Port La Joye, rendered a complaint on July 6 about the insulting manner of his dismissal, and in the ensuing lawsuit was vindicated by Dubuisson.

Incensed, Roma appealed for justice to de Pensens, the garrison commander, and to Maurepas, the Minister in France. He declaimed, "Dubuisson embarrasses me without ceasing, without missing the slightest occasion to sink a dagger in my heart."[18] De Pensens had just returned from two years in France, and soon allied himself with Roma, earning these words of praise from the beleaguered director: "It is so new to me in this country to hear the language of a man of honour, peace, wisdom and justice, and to hear sentiments favourable to my establishment...." Roma then continued his letter in a logical, if lengthy, refutation of the judgement.[19]

This correspondence bore fruit. In May 1734, Maurepas advised St. Ovide and Le Normant (respectively governor and financial commissary of Louisbourg, two officials who quarrelled incessantly, even though their names were so frequently bracketed) that Dubuisson "must not recur more complaints" and must favour Roma's settlement: a ministerial rap on the knuckles for the sub-delegate.[20] Dubuisson was moved to defend himself. "I did all I could to reconcile the two parties," he wrote, insisting that his lawsuit was "merely following the usual rules of justice." But he was being overly optimistic when he asserted, "This director [Roma] has now recovered from his animosity towards me and we are living in harmony together and will continue to do so as far as I am concerned. I am convinced the success of the Company will do much for the settlement of the island."[21]

A leader of men for many years, de Pensens submitted that had he been in Dubuisson's shoes, he could have handled the affair more efficiently, without involving St. Ovide, Le Normant, Caradec, and the Minister of the Marine. And he concurred with Roma's poor opinion of the Abbé de Bierne, "... a young scamp, more suited to a seminary than to the direction of souls. When left on their own," he continued, "these gentlemen start to act like little bishops. ... if anyone resists them, it is taken as sacrilege."[22] The priest's future career would seem to reinforce this unflattering view. He was sent to the Indian village of Malagawatch in Isle Royale, but soon went back to France, unable to learn the customs or language of the Mi'kmaq.

By the autumn of 1734, the quarrel between Roma and Dubuisson had blown over, although nine years later Roma was to demonstrate he had neither forgotten nor forgiven it.

Meanwhile, trouble was brewing in France among the shareholders of the Company of the East of Isle St. Jean. Gold was not flowing into their coffers from the New World. Neither were they placated by reports of roads, wheat crops, and log cabins — they wanted profits and they wanted them immediately. They sent support from France to Trois Rivières for only one year, and they were ready to seize upon any excuse to be exonerated from long-term investments. Roma had neglected the Company's fishermen, they complained to the Minister. He had made ill-advised journeys to Quebec and the Indies. He had spent far too much time and money on the settlement itself. In addition, his arrogance had destroyed enthusiasm and rebuffed his subordinates. For these reasons, no Company vessels would sail to Isle St. Jean in 1734.[23]

Dismayed, Roma had recourse to his pen, producing the table of works already mentioned. He enclosed these documents in a joint letter to St. Ovide, Le Normant, and de Pensens.[24] Through the high-flown prose and adamant self-righteousness of Roma's style emerges his bitter disillusionment with his partners, for his grand design was being thwarted by men of little minds and grasping souls, men with no concept of the adverse conditions under which he worked. The failure of his settlement, he claimed, would discourage future entrepreneurs.

De Pensens agreed. Too perturbed to be diplomatic, he wrote to the Minister in October 1734:

> I assure you, my Lord, it is unfortunate for Isle St. Jean that the investors of this Company are so easily disheartened .... I have seen and examined their cause of complaint and all I could find was a false pretext for abandoning their activities at the exact time when they might have started to reap the fruit of their labours. I have to give credit to a director who has done more in one year than M. de St. Pierre's company did all the time it was on the island .... In my opinion this is the only company out of all those which have set themselves up in this area which could have produced a profit if the investors had continued to send the necessary assistance to their director.[25]

De Pensens' conclusions must be taken seriously: his knowledge of colonial life was based on thirty-six years of varied and arduous duty in Placentia, Acadia, Isle Royale, and Isle St. Jean.[26]

Le Normant, who had visited Trois Rivières in the summer, added his words of commendation: "Sieur Roma acts his best and with attention and practical economy ... the roads which he made in the woods have cost very little."[27] Roma himself indignantly denied the accusations of the French merchants, while three of his principal employees certified, "we ... know no one who is at enmity with M. Roma or who has any just cause for complaint against him." Roma pleaded for the payment of only half of the arrears (which altogether amounted to 77,497 *livres*), a sum which would enable him to at least complete his settlement.[28]

But all to no avail. The following spring the shareholders were grumbling to the Minister about Roma's thirty leagues of roads, for which they claimed the fishermen had been employed, thereby depriving the Company of its rightful gains in salt cod. They also deplored an unprofitable voyage to Martinique, and the loss at sea of the *Michel Marie*, whose late departure for France from Trois Rivières in December 1733 had been entirely Roma's fault, since the crew had been delayed by him for "works of the land."

Although the Minister assumed his well-worn role of peacemaker, the investors flatly refused to send any more ships to Trois Rivières.[29] They even tried to return the establishments to the King's domain, an offer Louis XV declined to accept, having "no occasion to make any use of them, the island not being well enough established for it to be convenient to fix a port there at present."[30]

The Minister urged St. Ovide and Le Normant to continue their encouragement of the settlement, assuming that Roma would survive on the profits from the fishery, together with the goods still in his stores. Fortunately Isle St. Jean as a whole enjoyed a good harvest in 1735.[31]

A year later Cottard and the other partners in France were harping on the same refrain. They wanted to abandon the enterprise and place all the blame on Roma, who "did not wish to restrain himself to a few simple or narrow things" — like profits — "and elevated himself to .... visionary aspect." Having admonished their refractory colleague against incurring new expenses on their account, they proposed turning the concession over to Roma and a new Company, should one appear.[32]

This latter suggestion motivated Roma to leave Trois Rivières in the care of his children and a few servants early in November 1736. He travelled to Louisbourg, where he embarked upon the King's vessel *Le Profond*, with two of his employees and a family from his settlement who wished to go back to France.[33] By May of 1737, all the rights on the concession had been ceded to Roma, who thus became the sole proprietor. He would remain as commandant under the King's commission, with the blessing of the Minister of the Marine and the promise of support (moral if not financial) from the Louisbourg officials.[34]

Returning to Louisbourg in July on *Le Héros*, he spent a few days there, reregistering his letter of concession,[35] obtaining flour from the King's stores,[36] and — in typical Roma fashion — becoming embroiled in a domestic tangle.[37] Again the Father Superior of the Recollets, Zacarie Caradec, saw fit to poke his clerical nose into Roma's business, this time on behalf of two servant girls whom Roma had brought from La Rochelle in France, and had lodged temporarily with some respectable Louisbourg citizens. Certain other citizens, less amiably inclined, decided to alleviate the servant shortage by offering the girls employment, and were unscrupulous enough to enlist the aid of Caradec, whose hostility towards Roma must have been common knowledge. The priest and the French girls went from door to door spreading slanders about the Company director. This contributed to the defection of a cooper "whom I had brought over," Roma wrote, "and who was indispensible to me both for making and maintaining the barrels for my spirits, water, and beer, and for making wooden buckets."

Another item of business in Louisbourg was the choice of four *engagés* from the motley crew of *faux saulniers* (salt smugglers) transported

WOMEN BAKING IN TYPICAL 1700S DRESS

TYPICAL DRESS OF 1700S FRENCH COLONIAL WORKERS

from France every year. It was an indication of the decline of Roma's fortunes that to till his soil he had to make use of convicts, ruffians to whom the colonies were the only alternative to the living death of the galleys.

When Roma arrived at Trois Rivières, he found that all had not gone smoothly in the past few twenty-four months. "During my absence the lives of my family and my employees were placed in jeopardy by various perils. However, they were lucky enough to escape with no more than a certain amount of suffering and mental stress" — a subject on which one wishes Roma had chosen to exercise his usual verbosity. Perhaps he was referring to the fire in the early autumn of 1736, which had destroyed the crops in the more thickly settled areas of Isle St. Jean, placing many of the inhabitants in danger of starvation.[38] "My son had to eat part of his seed grain during a period of dearth," Roma recorded. In spite of this, the harvest of wheat and oats was ample, although the peas did not do well.

On his return, two of Roma's employees got married. He planned to establish them in a concession of their own, and with paternalistic fervour hoped this would encourage others to follow their example. How else to people this wilderness?

In the autumn he cleared more land and forecast greater harvests for 1738. But he was hampered by the mischief-making servant girls, who abetted three more employees not only in desertion, but in the theft of a fully equipped boat used for haying. (Hay came from the meadows around Rivière des Esturgeons.) This untoward reduction in his work force compelled Roma to negotiate for winter provisions at St. Pierre. "In addition," he lamented, "my children and I have had to work as hard as the last of my employees, with the result that we are now completely worn out."

At this time he must have felt keenly the loss of a valued ally and friend. De Pensens had gone to France in 1736, ostensibly on leave, but actually in such poor health that he retired in April 1737, and died a few months later. Instead Roma placed his trust on Le Normant, petitioning him to soundly reprimand the servant girls, and to bring the Father Superior to a due sense of his "crime against charity and all the laws."

Despite these misfortunes, Roma's faith in the future still burned brightly. In October he told the Minister that with the loan of fifty quintals of flour and the promise of six more convicts the following year, "I would dare swear on my own head that in very little time I could have the whole of Isle St. Jean flourishing."

THESE PHOTOGRAPHS SHOW THE BUILDINGS CONSTRUCTED ON THE ROMA SITE IN 2004

DETAILS OF 1700S PIQUET ARCHITECTURE. NOTE THE VERTICAL LOGS, SMALL PANES OF GLASS, SHUTTERS AND SMALL DORMERS.

Of Mice and Shipwrecks (1738–1743)

It would be many years before Isle St. Jean prospered as Roma hoped, and his optimistic view of the future was dealt a bitter blow in the summer of 1738. The farmers of Isle St. Jean were expecting an abundant harvest, when the land was laid waste by an extraordinary plague of field mice. Wheat, oats, barley, hay — everything fell before the voracious rodents. Acadia came to the rescue with 600 bushels of seed grain. Dubuisson distributed flour, peas, guns, shot and powder, to the despairing habitants, as well as spending 1,100 *livres* from his own pocket: a fact that helped to counterbalance Roma's vilification of the sub-delegate.[39]

"We have received no news of M. Roma for some time now," Le Normant wrote to the Minister in October. "We know he did a great deal of work for his settlement last autumn and the following spring, but we have since learned indirectly that his land has also been ravaged by field mice."[40]

It had. But Roma did not intend for it to happen again, and therefore devoted himself to a study of the mice, carefully noting their appearance, eating habits, and remarkable fecundity. He described how the tiny creatures emerged from the woods, spread in a grey blanket over the fields, and finally tumbled into the sea to drown by the thousands. He attributed their overwhelming numbers to two successive winters of heavy snow, which had protected them from their natural enemies, and said they could be controlled only by clearing more land and by destroying their nests at the edges of the cultivated fields.[41]

Crops were bountiful in 1739. Roma's problems, however, were too deep-rooted to be solved by one good harvest, so he started negotiations to sell the *St. Jean* to Pierre Maurice, a Louisbourg merchant, in exchange for two negroes and two negresses.[42] The new year brought further trouble. On January 28, 1740, "a woman in my service set fire to my building, which destroyed it with all my livestock."[43] How? Why? We are not told. In February Roma travelled to Port la Joye seeking to replenish his depleted food supplies. While there, he had an audience with the new Lieutenant de Roi, Du Chambon, and an old enemy, Dubuisson. He put before them the proposal that three of his *faux saulniers*, or convicts, whose time expired in August, should be ordered to

ISLANDERS IN 1700S COSTUME:
THREE RIVERS ROMA INC. BOARD OF DIRECTORS 2004

remain long enough to harvest his grain, for which he would pay each of them a bonus of 10 *écus*.

Bourville (acting governor of Louisbourg) and Bigot (Le Normant's replacement) paid Roma a visit early in the summer of 1740, about which Bigot later commented, "Sieur Roma leads a miserable life there (Trois Rivières) lacking everything; his land is not enough for him to subsist with his family. He proposes to fish by boat at Pointe de l'Est, but I doubt if he will succeed, not having any advance payments."[44]

In July, Roma, his convicts, and Dubuisson happened to gather at St. Pierre, where Dubuisson gave the required order concerning the harvest. Accompanied by a crew of two, Roma then departed for Léon Fautoux's house in Louisbourg to complete the sale of the *St. Jean*.[45] Although the records are scanty for this period, apparently Roma's financial difficulties necessitated an extended stay at the fortress. Not one to be idle, he used the time to form a fishing crew, but unfortunately was shipwrecked in January 1741, losing the vessel and its cargo. Refusing to admit defeat, Roma sought an audience with Bigot, the financial commissary. The latter promised to stand surety for a loan of 1,000 *livres* to be repaid in two years, with which Roma proposed to construct a twenty-five-ton *goelette* (schooner).[46]

Before leaving Louisbourg, Roma received a communication from his son to the effect that Dubuisson had allowed two of the three *faux saulniers* to abandon last year's harvest and had also incited other labourers to desert. This, coupled with the rainy weather, had decreased the yield of grain by 30 to 40 quintals. There was bread at Trois Rivières only until the first days of June.

Roma hurriedly borrowed 25 quintals of flour ("which I shall pay back next year") from the Louisbourg stores,[47] fired off a *memoire* of complaint to the governor (the one-legged Du Quesnel) and Bigot, and was home by June 17, after an absence of nearly a year. Desperately short of cloth because of his shipwreck, he asked the Minister to send from

France a bale of dry-goods valued at 500 *livres*. Payment? The flour and peas of next year's crop.[48] The debts were mounting ominously.

That summer Roma composed "an ample letter" to Dubuisson, "representing to him with civility the latest wrongs he had caused." Oddly enough, its delivery was entrusted to a Recollet priest, Ambroise Aubré. The sub-delegate did not reply directly, but in a series of iudgements condemned Roma to replace equipment wilfully smashed by the convicts, and to pay the three felons who had remained for the harvest an outrageously high salary, far more than they could have earned as free men. It would seem that Dubuisson also instigated the desertion of the Duboc family ("bad lots," according to Roma), and of three more *faux saulniers*, "who made the rest of my strength for the outside work," and who soon lodged complaints of their ex-master with the sub-delegate.

"Work was their genuine grievance," said Roma tartly. Leaving his daughter Marie Anne dangerously sick, he sailed to Port la Joye with a written request to imprison the runaways until the full weight of the law could order them back to Trois Rivières. Du Chambon refused to read it. Dubuisson, even with the help of his spectacles, had trouble deciphering Roma's handwriting, an understandable predicament. Without acceding to the request, the two of them left for St. Pierre, Roma in hot pursuit. There he learned that the deserters had been permitted to live with various habitants, and were as busy spreading slanders about his good name as they were working in the fields. Roma was not alone in his difficulties with French convicts. In 1741 and 1742 the Louisbourg officials tactfully requested the Minister keep these *faux saulniers* in France, as they were scoundrels, thieves, and vagrants — a blemish on the colony until, as frequently happened, they fled to the New England states via British privateers.[49]

Eventually Roma did obtain a favourable hearing from Du Chambon, although this did not stop him from addressing a voluminous *memoire* of complaint against Dubuisson to the Minister in 1743. "The greatest mishap for a habitant isolated as I am ... is to lose his people to the point of not being able to provide for ploughing, for seed, for the business of hay, or that of the harvest, because the result is his ruin ...." The blame for this mishap Roma laid at Dubuisson's door.

On March 25, 1744, Dubuisson died. He was buried at eleven o'clock the next morning near the black cross in the Port la Joye cemetery, survived only by his unmarried daughter Louise.[50] The officiating clergyman described him as a man of nobility, and certainly he had laboured long and hard for the French settlers, under incredibly difficult and discouraging circumstances. Death thus brought an end to the feud that had rankled for twelve years between Roma and Dubuisson.

ACTOR PORTRAYING ROMA

War (1744–1748)

The early 1740s were years of relative prosperity in Isle St. Jean, years of good harvest and slow migration of Acadians from the mainland. But war was soon to disrupt this peaceful pattern, for France was becoming far too powerful commercially for the peace of mind of the English.

In May 1744, Du Quesnel, the governor at Louisbourg, was alerted to the outbreak of hostilities between the two countries; the same month he warned Isle St. Jean to stand on its guard. After Du Quesnel's death in October, Du Chambon became governor, more or less by accident. A young French officer named Du Vivier took soldiers from Port la Joye on a fruitless campaign to Annapolis in August, then returned to command the remaining twenty-man garrison throughout the winter.

A mixed bag of New Englanders and British succeeded in capturing the impregnable fortress of Louisbourg in June 1745 after a forty-six-day siege — Du Chambon may well have regretted his hasty promotion. Once its capture became a certainty, Pepperrell dispatched an expedition to "St. John's Island." The shabby houses of Port la Joye were gutted, although Du Vivier and his soldiers killed or wounded nine of the invaders.[51]

At Trois Rivières, there was no resistance. Roma claimed "at the time I had not been informed of the war and had been surprised by the enemy,"[52] a statement difficult to believe in view of all the above manoeuvres spread over more than a year, unless he had become a recluse. (This is a possibility. During his time on the island, he never attended the weddings and baptisms that were the focus of the social life in Port la Joye and St. Pierre.[53]) It is equally difficult to believe he would have surrendered his establishment without at least token resistance, unless he had been taken by surprise.

On that fateful day in June, there were only eight people at Trois Rivières, including Roma himself and two of his children. Their sole weapon of defence was a six-pound cannon, more suitable for ceremonial occasions than for repelling an enemy attack. So it must have been with deep anxiety that Roma watched the billowing white sails of a foreign ship approach across the blue waters of the bay. Offshore, its canvas was furled. The anchor splashed into the sea. When a boat was lowered, laden with plunder-hungry New Englanders who had no reason to love the French, Roma fled to the shelter of the woods with his son and daughter, two servants, and three valets.

VISITORS TRY ON 1700S CLOTHING AT FÊTE ROMA 2004

From the trees, he must have watched the provincials haul his precious bushels of wheat and peas, his tools, and livestock to their ship. He must have seen them set fire to his houses, barns, and workshops. Amid the clouds of blue smoke and the crackle of greedy orange flames, his dream was levelled to the ground.

Surfeited with loot and destruction, the New Englanders departed. Only then could Roma emerge from his hiding place to discover the full extent of the disaster. He was left without food or shelter, his crops and gardens trampled, and his buildings reduced to charred and smouldering ruins. He would later estimate the damage at 50,000 *livres*, enumerating his losses complete to the last chicken.[54]

A lesser man would have shaken the island's mud from his feet and sailed away on the first favourable wind, vowing never to return to such a fated and thankless place. Not so Roma. With his little band of tired and hungry refugees, he travelled on foot to St. Pierre, along the rough trail blazed nearly thirteen years ago. For twelve months Roma remained on the island, presumably living on his concession at St. Pierre.

Two letters written to the French Minister in 1749 and 1752 furnish an account of Roma's activities during that year.[55] (It should be remembered that in this correspondence Roma was pleading for permission to return to Isle St. Jean, and would certainly have presented his conduct in the best light possible.) According to these letters, Roma prevented the Mi'kmaq from shifting allegiance to the English, and exhorted the inhabitants to stand fast in their loyalty to the King. This was no easy task, since well-founded rumours of mass deportation flew back and forth between Louisbourg and Isle St. Jean, and it was generally known that 4,000 Louisbourg residents had been shipped off to France in July.

With a distinct and characteristic lack of modesty, Roma suggested that if those in high places had listened to his advice, Louisbourg could have been retaken during the winter, when sickness decimated the English garrison. One-hundred-and-seventy English had been killed in the siege. Eight-hundred-and-ninety died, mostly of scurvy, between December and April, living and dead lying together in the damp and verminous barracks.[56] In June, France did send a fleet to recapture the fortress, under the Duc d'Anville, but his men died like flies from scurvy and typhus, and his ships vanished in the vicious storms off Sable Island. He died of apoplexy (poison, said his crew), and the battered remnants of his armada limped back to France, without ever firing a shot. God is on our side, exulted the pious — and relieved — New Englanders.[57]

Having risked his life in the King's service, and having been personally menaced by the English in Isle St. Jean, Roma took refuge in Quebec in June 1746. He stayed there for more than three years. For one known as the Commander of the Company of the East of Isle St. Jean, it must have been a grievous comedown to be employed as a mere cleric in the stores by Hocquart, the financial commissary. Even there, Roma could not be satisfied to do things the conventional way. As one of his contemporaries stated, "He [Roma] worked very hard, but in a different manner than that established in our offices, a manner which was confused and so extraordinary that it necessitated having several of the receipt, expenditure, and balance books done again by Sieur Estebe, the storekeeper."[58]

Roma's family now comes to the fore. His wife, Marie Magdeleine Moreau, remains an elusive figure, never mentioned directly in any of her husband's correspondence and absent from Trois Rivières for the censuses of 1734, 1735, and 1739.[59] Perhaps she never lived there permanently. At least three of Roma's children were in Quebec with him. His son Jean Pierre Michel was a "writer for the service of the King in this city."[60] In 1750 he became ill and died there. In February 1748, Roma's daughter Marie Anne attended the baptism of Marie, a day-old baby of a slave of her father's, and in July she witnessed the donation of the child to a Quebec merchant, Fleury de la Gorgendière.[61] Marie Anne lived at Louisbourg from 1750 to 1758, marrying Jean Du Chambon, a son of the ex-Lieutenant de Roi of Isle St. Jean, in 1757.[62] Also in Isle Royale at that time was her younger brother Jean Baptiste, who could not have inherited his father's anti-clerical bias, since he was assisting the well-loved

DESCENDANTS OF JEAN PIERRE ROMA'S SON JEAN BAPTISTE
WITH ACTOR ROBERT ARSENAULT AS ROMA AT FÊTE ROMA 2004

Abbé Maillard at his Indian mission on Chapel Island.[63]

The Treaty of Aix-la-Chapelle, signed in October 1748, was more a truce than a genuine peace treaty, allowing a breathing space for England and France to prepare for the next struggle. Its terms had been public since April, an example *par excellence* of the futility of war: "the places taken during the war were mutually restored."[64] Hence Isle Royale and Isle St. Jean reverted to France.

In June 1748, the Minister urged the Quebec officials to encourage the passage of Acadians to Isle St. Jean as quickly as possible. Therefore troops and provisions were conveyed from Quebec to Port la Joye at the end of August,[65] and with them went another of Roma's sons, Jean Pierre Nicolas. As stores guard, his duties were to distribute supplies, merchandise, and munitions to the garrison, the habitants, and the Mi'kmaq. His formal instructions, written in Quebec by Hocquart on August 23, 1748, make it clear that the inhabitants were already known to him, presumably from the years that he had lived at Trois Rivières.[66]

Trapped at an office desk perusing columns of figures, Roma must have envied Nicolas his new job. But the situation was not totally hopeless, for the war was over and Louisbourg and Isle St. Jean were no longer in enemy hands. He, Jean Pierre Roma, still controlled the concession at Trois Rivières, where houses could be rebuilt, fishing boats launched again, and fresh crops sown. As the 1740s drew to a close, Roma's determination to return to his island home hardened into a sense of purpose that would direct the course of his life for many months to come.

Years of Exile (1749–1757)

With due ceremony, the French marched into Louisbourg and the English marched out. By the end of July 1749, the evacuees had been transported to the newly cleared townsite of Halifax, peopled largely by the dregs of the London slums. The business of running Louisbourg and its surrounding territories had been taken up by the new governor, Charles Des Herbiers, and his unpopular assistant, Jacques Prévost. Roma's position as commander of Trois Rivières was not as secure as he had assumed, for one of the first regulations of these officials proclaimed that lands conceded to former inhabitants must be occupied and developed within the year, or be reunited to the King's domain and granted to new landlords.[67] Two weeks later, on August 15, they wrote to the Minister: "M. Roma has an immense area of land at Trois Rivières. It is not fitting that the existence of this concession should prevent us from settling Acadians on this land."[68]

In November, Roma himself was in Louisbourg en route to Martinique, where he hoped to amass enough capital to rebuild Trois Rivières. (This was a reasonable prospect, for the Indies were prosperous as French Canada never was. By 1740 their annual exports to France amounted to 100 million *livres*.[69] It was a prosperity based on vast plantations of sugar canes and coffee bushes, and the labour of Negro slaves who were treated with incredible cruelty.)

Roma had planned for Nicolas to start the restoration of his settlement, but in August his son had been ousted from the position of stores guard by the appointment of a sub-delegate, François-Marie de Goutin.[70] Worried that Des Herbiers' regulation could cost him his concession, Roma begged for an extension on the basis of the money and labour he had lost by an accident of war, and on the governor's advice appealed to the Minister before embarking for the Indies.[71]

The sea voyage strengthened rather than weakened Roma's interest in the fate of Trois Rivières. In Martinique he was soon too busy writing about Isle St. Jean to be accumulating any capital. Between March and May 1750, he sent the new Minister of the Marine, Rouille, a number of letters, which accompanied successive installments of a plan for the development of Isle Royale and Isle St. Jean, a plan that would thwart forever English designs upon the islands. Principles, proofs, articles, and explanations were all numbered and annotated, page after page—more than "sixty days of work without respite."[72]

What was the gist of this monumental task? First, Roma cited some of the reasons that Acadians were reluctant to migrate to Isle St. Jean. They found it impossible to transport their livestock across the strait because of English corsairs. They experienced great difficulty in ridding the land of its massive trees, having been accustomed for generations to the open marshlands of the Minas Basin. Furthermore, they suffered from the ever-present threat of an enemy attack from which their sole protection was an inadequate and unruly garrison.

All these problems could be solved very simply, said Roma, by bringing in 6,000 militiamen, and by spreading them in forty-six districts along the entire coastline. Such a deployment would enable the inhabitants to communicate and trade with each other, to fish in safety, and, in case of danger, to assemble at any one point in twenty-four hours. He recommended that the troops, engaged for five years, should be healthy, anxious to make their fortune, and capable of hard work. So proud of their achievements would such troops be, and so devoted to the welfare of the island, that the Acadians would flock there with their sons and daughters — the latter hopefully catching the eyes and hearts of the busy militiamen in "a good number of marriages."[73] Thus King Louis's power would increase in Isle St. Jean and his reputation become so formidable to England that George II would hasten to cultivate friendship between the two countries.

How anxiously Roma must have awaited the mail packets in the vessels from France! Surely now his zeal for the King's service was incontestable and his return to Isle St. Jean imminent. But ship after ship came and went. He moved on to St. Domingue "in the hope of forming a society for the restoration of his concession."[74] In 1752 he wrote again to the Minister. Uncertain whether the 1749 regulation had already deprived him of his land, he humbled himself to plead for compensation that would allow him to reconstruct Trois Rivières, with the additional benefit of "some honourable post there."[75]

An "honourable post" was vacant. De Goutin, the sub-delegate, had died in January, leaving his bookkeeper Nicolas Deslongrais in charge of the stores, and the Minister asked Prévost whether Roma would be a suitable replacement. Late in November, Prévost replied. Because the 1749 regulation had been renewed, "the concession remains in the hands of the said Roma ... from the details I have given of M. Roma's losses ... you will decide what you may see fit to do for him, such as an annual or extraordinary allowance enabling him to rebuild his settlement." As for the position of sub-delegate, Prévost was adamant. He acknowledged Roma to be a man of spirit, talent, and experience, but added:

> his character is so caustic that it is to be feared he could not agree with anyone. In fact he is naturally inconstant and given to experiments and projects that might disturb the establishments of the habitants. Moreover, he is known in Isle St. Jean as a partial man, and one would be justly afraid to see him administer justice there. ... I doubt also whether he could or would settle himself at Port la Joye in such a mediocre position .... The position of storekeeper in Port la Joye cannot be left in better hands than those of M. Deslongrais, he performs his duties very wel l... and I beg you to grant him this post.[76]

Probably Prévost's advice was not totally disinterested, as he and Deslongrais may have indulged in shady business dealings together.[77] Certainly Prévost was universally disliked, being ill-mannered, untrustworthy, and vindictive.[78] The Minister, however, did not argue. Although Deslongrais was never appointed sub-delegate, he remained Warden of Stores until 1758. Prévost's suggestion of "an annual or extraordinary allowance" for Roma came to nothing, and without capital Roma was banished from Trois Rivières as surely as if by royal decree.

The final knell to Roma's hopes sounded on January 1, 1753, when the governor of Louisbourg pronounced that any concessions uninhabited by the first of May would be reunited to the King's domain.[79] Thus did an ungrateful government dismiss Roma's long years of service at Trois Rivières, his letters of entreaty, and his plans for Isle St. Jean.

Roma had no choice but to remain in the Indies, and by 1757 had become director of the domain of Guadeloupe.[80] But the days of the French empire were numbered. After a long siege, Louisbourg surrendered to the British in 1758. Quebec and Guadeloupe fell in 1759, the rest of Canada in 1760, Martinique in 1762. On the verge of bankruptcy, the European powers signed the Treaty of Paris in 1763. France had lost her vast North American territories, apart from the tiny islands of St. Pierre and Miquelon, and fishing rights off the coast of Newfoundland. She bargained successfully for Martinique and Guadeloupe, and kept the western half of St. Domingue. Throughout these tumultuous years, did Roma remain in Guadeloupe? Did he die in France, or was he buried under a tropical sun?

The answers to these questions are not known. Yet, wherever Roma lived out his last years, a part of him must always have remembered Trois Rivières — sails snapping in the cold Atlantic winds; waves lapping at the sandstone wharf; summer breezes rippling his wheat; smoke spiralling from the chimneys of his house — "a place which has cost me dearly and is therefore precious to me."[81]

Roma at Three Rivers
History of the Site Since 1750

Since the time of Jean Pierre Roma, the site of Trois Rivières has been home to other settlers and activities. In the early 1800s, brothers Angus and Hugh Macdonald operated a store and tavern here and built at least eight sailing ships. A. A. Macdonald, noted statesman and one of the Fathers of Confederation, was born here. And various land owners farmed the area.

In 1936 Parks Canada erected a monument honouring Jean Pierre Roma. During the summers of 1968, 1969, and 1970, archaeologists did extensive research on the site. Then, in 2003, a group of community volunteers united under the name Three Rivers Roma Inc. to develop the site more fully. In 2004 the site was officially named Roma at Three Rivers, two buildings in the style of Roma's time were built, nine kilometres of nature trails were cut out of 110 acres of provincially owned land, and the first celebration, Fête Roma 2004, drew crowds of over 1,200 people, including some of Roma's descendants.

Roma at Three Rivers now awaits you. You can get there by driving to the end of route 319 just north of Montague, or disembark at the wharf on the Montague River side of the property. You can explore the carefully signposted nature and heritage trails, enjoy the displays in the buildings, and take part in guided tours and historic re-enactments. The initial emphasis is on the history of Roma's time, but the Macdonald era also will be highlighted as the project grows. The buildings may be rented for private celebrations or you may picnic, stroll, enjoy the river views, ski, or snowshoe as the season allows.

For information about current programs at the site, visit
www.romapei.com

Endnotes

AC=Archives des Colonies
PAC=Public Archives of Canada

1. PAC, Archives des Colonies, C11B, Vol. 16, pp. 47–48.
2. PAC, AC, C11B, Vol. 20, pp. 162–164.
3. D. C. Harvey, *The French Regime in Prince Edward Island* (New York, 1970), pp. 66–68.
4. PAC, AC, B, Vol. 55-3, pp. 755–759.
5. PAC, AC, B, Vol. 55-3, pp. 722–729.
6. PAC, AC, B, Vol. 55-1, pp. 95–97.
7. PAC, AC, B, Vol. 57-2, pp. 406–407.
8. Blaine Adams, *The Construction and Occupation of the Barracks of the King's Bastion* (July 1971), pp. 119–120. Manuscript on file National Historic Parks and Sites Branch, Louisbourg, National Historic Park.
9. PAC, AC, MGl, G2, Vol. 191, pp. 12, 12v, 13.
10. PAC, Archives de la France de l'Outre Mer, G3, Carton 2038.
11. PAC, AC, C11B, Vol. 16, pp. 41–59, 70–100.
12. PAC, AC, C11B, Vol. 17, p. 127.
13. PAC, AC, B. Vol. 59-2, pp. 396–401.
14. *Dictionary of Canadian Biography,* Vol. III (Toronto), pp. 532–533.
15. PAC, AC, C11B, Vol. 13, pp. 79–80.
16. The story of the two priests is found in the following: PAC, Archives de la Marine, C7, #282, Dossier Personnel de Roma, Memoire Canada 1743, pp. 4, 6–7.
17. PAC, AC, C11B, Vol. 14, p. 222.
18. PAC, AC, C11B, Vol. 14, p. 263.
19. PAC, AC, C11B, Vol. 14, pp. 221–234.
20. PAC, AC, B, Vol. 61-2, pp. 380–381.
21. PAC, AC, C11B, Vol. 13, pp. 81–84.
22. PAC, AC, C11B, Vol. 16, pp. 34–40.
23. PAC, AC, B, Vol. 61-2, pp. 376–378. PAC, AC, C11B, Vol. 16, pp. 174–178.
24. PAC, AC, C11B, Vol. 16, pp. 60–69 (translated in full in Harvey, op. cit., pp. 80–84).
25. PAC, AC, C11B, Vol. 16, pp. 34–40.
26. *Dictionary of Canadian Biography,* Vol. II (Toronto), pp. 218–220.
27. PAC, AC, B, Vol. 62, pp. 61–63.
28. PAC, AC, C11B, Vol. 16, pp. 174–178.

29. PAC, AC, B, Vol. 63-2, pp. 429–431.
30. PAC, AC, B, Vol. 62, pp. 61–63.
31. PAC, AC, C11B, Vol. 17, p. 125.
32. PAC, AC, B, Vol. 64-4, pp. 721–727.
33. PAC, AC, C11B, Vol. 18, pp. 106–108. PAC, AC, B, Vol. 65-4, pp. 807–808.
34. PAC, AC, B, Vol. 65-4, pp. 887–888.
35. PAC, AC, MGI, G2, Carton 190, Part 2, Folios 2–5.
36. PAC, AC, C11B, Vol. 19, pp. 75–77.
37. The events and quotations in the rest of this section are covered in the following reference: PAC, AC, C11B, Vol. 19, pp. 71–74, 174–179.
38. Harvey, op. cit., pp. 102–103.
39. Harvey, op. cit., pp. 104–105.
40. PAC, AC, C11B, Vol. 19, pp. 31–41.
41. PAC, AC, Vol. 29, Part 2, pp. 352–356.
42. PAC, G3, Vol. 2046-1, folio 175 (Reel F-540).
43. The events from 1740 to 1743 are related in the following: Archives de la Marine, C7, #282, Dossier Personnel de Roma, Memoire Canada 1743, pp. 7–13.
44. Documents pour Servir à l'Histoire de l'Isle Saint Jean, UPEI Library, Vol. 3 (1738–1749), p. 23.
45. PAC, Archives Départementales, Charente Maritime, MG6, A2(a), Series B, p. 60 (folios 25v–26).
46. PAC, AC, C11B, Vol. 20, pp. 162–164.
47. PAC, AC, C 11B, Vol. 23, pp. 165–168.
48. PAC, AC, C11B, Vol. 23, pp. 165–168.
49. Documents pour Servir à l'Histoire de l'Isle Saint Jean, UPEI Library, Vol. 3 (1738–1749), pp. 45, 56.
50. PAC, AC, MG1, G1, Vol. 411, p. 267.
51. Harvey, op. cit., pp. 110–111.
52. Archives de la Marine, C7, #282, Dossier Personnel de Roma, Lettre à Monseigneur Rouillé, 1752.
53. PAC, AC, MG1, G1, Vol. 411, pp. 164–268.
54. Archives de la Marine, C7, #282, Dossier Personnel de Roma, Lettre à Monseigneur Rouillé, 1752. PAC, AC, C. 11B, Vol. 32, pp. 245–251.
55. These two letters are found in Roma's Dossier Personnel, Archives de la Marine, C7, #282.
56. J. S. McLennan, *Louisbourg from its Foundation to its Fall* (Sydney, 1957), pp. 173–174.

57. Thomas H. Raddall, *Halifax Warden of the North* (Toronto, 1971), pp. 11–15.
58. PAC, AC, C11B, Vol. 32, pp. 245–251.
59. PAC, AC, MG1, G1, Vol. 466, Part 2, pp. 243–273 (1734, 1735). PAC, AC, MG1, Vol. 466, No. 44 (Reel F 768) (1739).
60. Archives nationales du Québec, Acte de Sépulture de Jean Pierre Michel Roma, 11 janvier 1750, à l'Hôtel-Dieu.
61. Archives nationales du Québec, Donation par Jean Pierre Roma, 15 juillet 1748, Acte du Notaire J. C. Panet.
62. PAC, Archives de la France de l'Outre Mer, G3, Carton 2045.
63. Census by the Sieur de la Roque, Public Archives Report, 1905, II, Appendix A. p. 36. Halifax County: Court of Probate. Vol. 1, Pg. 250 ff, Will of Abbé Maillard (microfilm copy at Public Archives of Nova Scotia).
64. McLennan, op. cit., p. 181.
65. Harvey, op. cit., p. 121.
66. Archives nationales du Québec, Ordonnances des Intendants, 1748, NF-2, 35, Folios 56v–59v.
67. Louisbourg Archives, 1 août 1749, DesHerbiers et Prévost, A.N., A.C., F3, 50 456–456v.
68. PAC, AC, C11B, Vol. 28, pp. 10–15.
69. W. J. Eccles, *France in America* (New York, 1972), p. 158.
70. PAC, AC, C11B, Vol. 28, pp. 218–221.
71. Archives de la Marine, C7, #282, Dossier Personnel de Roma, Lettre au Ministre, 17 novembre 1749.
72. PAC, AC, C11B, Vol. 29, Folios 356–427v. PAC, AC, C11C, Vol. 16, Part I, pp. 122–191.
73. R. H. Casgrain, *Une Seconde Acadie* (Québec, 1894), pp. 212–214.
74. Archives de la Marine, C7, #282, Dossier Personnel de Roma, Lettre à Monseigneur Rouillé, 1752.
75. Ibid.
76. PAC, AC, C11B, Vol. 32, pp. 245–251.
77. *Dictionary of Canadian Biography*, Vol. III (Toronto), pp. 184–185.
78. McLennan, op. cit., pp. 231–232.
79. Louisbourg Archives, 1 janvier 1753, De Raymond et Prévost, A.N., A.C., F3, 50 496.
80. PAC, AC, C11B, Vol. 19, p. 179.
81. Ibid.

Joel Ross

Jill MacLean

Born in England in 1941, Jill MacLean moved to Nova Scotia with her family in 1950. After receiving her Bachelor of Science with honours from Dalhousie University, she worked at the Fisheries Research Board in Halifax, in Sydney City Hospital, and in the Biology Department of Mount Allison University. During the four years she lived in Prince Edward Island, she researched Jean Pierre Roma's settlement at Trois Rivières; her monograph was published by the PEI Heritage Foundation in 1977. Later, she completed a Master's in Theological Studies at the Atlantic School of Theology, and began writing poetry. Her first collection, *The Brevity of Red*, was published in 2003. She now lives in Bedford with her partner, Mike, and is working on a book for their grandson, Stuart.